GET THE ANSWERS! History

Q&A ABOUT THE PLYMOUTH COLONY

By Benjamin Proudfit

INVESTIGATE!

Enslow PUBLISHING

Please visit our website, www.enslow.com. For a free color catalog of all our high-quality books, call toll free 1-800-398-2504 or fax 1-877-980-4454.

Library of Congress Cataloging-in-Publication Data

Names: Proudfit, Benjamin, author.
Title: Q & A about the Plymouth Colony / Benjamin Proudfit.
Other titles: Questions and answers about the Plymouth Colony
Description: Buffalo, New York : Enslow Publishing, [2026] | Series: Get the answers! : History | Includes bibliographical references and index. | Audience: Grades 2-3
Identifiers: LCCN 2024059880 (print) | LCCN 2024059881 (ebook) | ISBN 9781978544406 (library binding) | ISBN 9781978544390 (paperback) | ISBN 9781978544413 (ebook)
Subjects: LCSH: Pilgrims (New Plymouth Colony)–Miscellanea–Juvenile literature. | Massachusetts–History–New Plymouth, 1620-1691–Juvenile literature.
Classification: LCC F68 .P96 2026 (print) | LCC F68 (ebook) | DDC 974.4/02–dc23/eng/20250214
LC record available at https://lccn.loc.gov/2024059880
LC ebook record available at https://lccn.loc.gov/2024059881

Published in 2026 by
Enslow Publishing
2544 Clinton Street
Buffalo, NY 14224

Designer: Andrea Davison-Bartolotta
Editor: Kristen Nelson

Photo credits: Cover, pp. 1, 17 The Miriam and Ira D. Wallach Division of Art, Prints and Photographs: Picture Collection/ NYPL Digital Collections; series art (question mark backgrounds) Darcraft/Shutterstock.com; pp. 5, 14 Everett Collection/Shutterstock.com; p. 6 File:George-Henry-Boughton-Pilgrims- Going-To-Church.jpg/Wikimedia Commons; p. 7 Joseph Sohm/Shutterstock.com; p. 8 File:Embarkation of the Pilgrims.jpg/Wikimedia Commons; p. 9 File:Mayflower II galley.jpg/Wikimedia Commons; p. 10 Library of Congress; p. 11 PorcupenWorks/Shutterstock.com; p. 12 Igal Shkolnik/Shutterstock.com; p. 13 File:The Mayflower Compact 1620 cph.3g07155.jpg/Wikimedia Commons; p. 15 Jaclyn Vernace/Shutterstock.com; p. 16 National Gallery of Art; p. 18 AF Fotografie/Alamy Stock Photo; p. 19 Michael Gordon/Shutterstock.com; p. 20 Anneka/Shutterstock.com; p. 21 (beans) pundapanda/Shutterstock.com; p. 21 (corn bread)RFondren Photography/Shutterstock.com; p. 21 (goose) Mironov Vladimir/Shutterstock.com; p. 21 (lobster) Spalnic/Shutterstock.com; p. 21 (shellfish)denio109/Shutterstock.com; p. 21 (squash) Robyn Mackenzie/ Shutterstock.com; p. 21 (venison) hlphoto/Shutterstock.com; p. 22 nyker/Shutterstock.com; p. 23 Ja Crispy/ Shutterstock.com; p. 24 ZU_09/iStockphoto.com; p. 25 Kellie Sheridan/Shutterstock.com; p. 26 Universal Images Group North America LLC/Alamy Stock Photo; p. 27 File:Philip King of Mount Hope by Paul Revere.jpeg/Wikimedia Commons; p. 29 (inset) Scott K Baker/Shutterstock.com; p. 29 Alexander Sviridov/Shutterstock.com.

Printed in the United States of America

CPSIA compliance information: Batch #CS26ENS: For further information contact Enslow Publishing, at 1-800-398-2504.

CONTENTS

A Colony of Firsts....4

Getting Started....6

Arriving in New England....10

Native Neighbors....17

Self-Sufficiency....22

Growing Colonies....26

Massachusetts Colony....28

Glossary....30

For More Information....31

Index....32

Words in the glossary appear in **bold** type the first time they are used in the text.

A COLONY OF FIRSTS

Plymouth Colony was the first colonial settlement in **New England**. It was founded by English settlers who wanted a place where they could practice their religion, or faith, freely. This founding of a community based on common religious ideas paved the way for other similar settlements in New England.

Today, the Pilgrims, the *Mayflower*, and the harvest feast they **celebrated** with the Wampanoag people are remembered around Thanksgiving every year. Still, there's so much more to learn about this colony!

Plymouth Colony only existed on its own for about 70 years. Because it was such an early colony it had a big effect on New England!

GETTING STARTED

QUESTION 1

How did Plymouth Colony come about?

ANSWER

In England, only one religion was allowed: the Church of England. A group called the Puritans split from the church. Another group, the Separatists, came from the Puritans. They wanted to found a colony built around their religious ideas.

The Separatists went into business with investors. These people paid for their passage to North America and supplies to help them start their colony.

QUESTION 2

Who was aboard the *Mayflower*?

ANSWER

The *Mayflower* is the ship the Separatists took to North America. When the ship left England on September 6, 1620, there were about 40 Separatists aboard. The investors gathered about 60 other English colonists too.

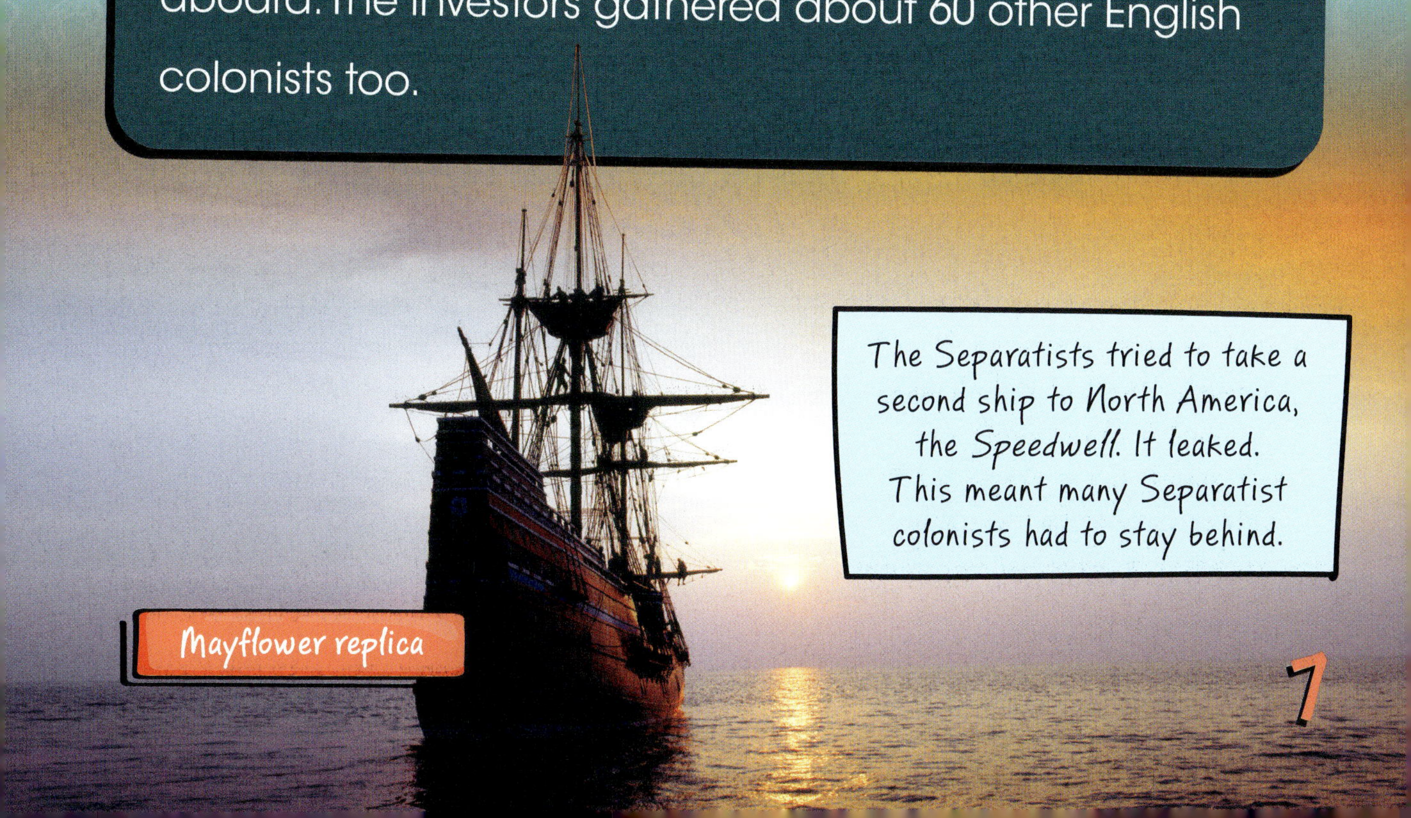

Mayflower replica

The Separatists tried to take a second ship to North America, the *Speedwell*. It leaked. This meant many Separatist colonists had to stay behind.

QUESTION 3

Why are they called "Pilgrims" today?

ANSWER

The word pilgrim means a person who travels for a long time, commonly for religious reasons. Those aboard the *Mayflower* didn't call themselves pilgrims. But, in writings from the time, at least one Separatist did. He used a lowercase "p."

Calling those who traveled on the *Mayflower* Pilgrims—with a capital "P"—started in the 1800s. Today, it's a general word used to talk about anyone who lived in Plymouth Colony early on.

QUESTION 4

What was the journey on the Mayflower like?

ANSWER

It was dark, wet, cold, and **cramped**. It took about 66 days to get from England to North America. For all that time, the Pilgrims traveled in the **cargo** hold of the ship.

This shows what the Pilgrims' cargo area may have looked like.

ARRIVING IN NEW ENGLAND

QUESTION 5

Did they reach the place they wanted to?

ANSWER

No. They had a **patent** to settle near the Hudson River in present-day New York. The colony of Virginia reached that far north at the time. However, storms and other problems stopped the Pilgrims from getting there.

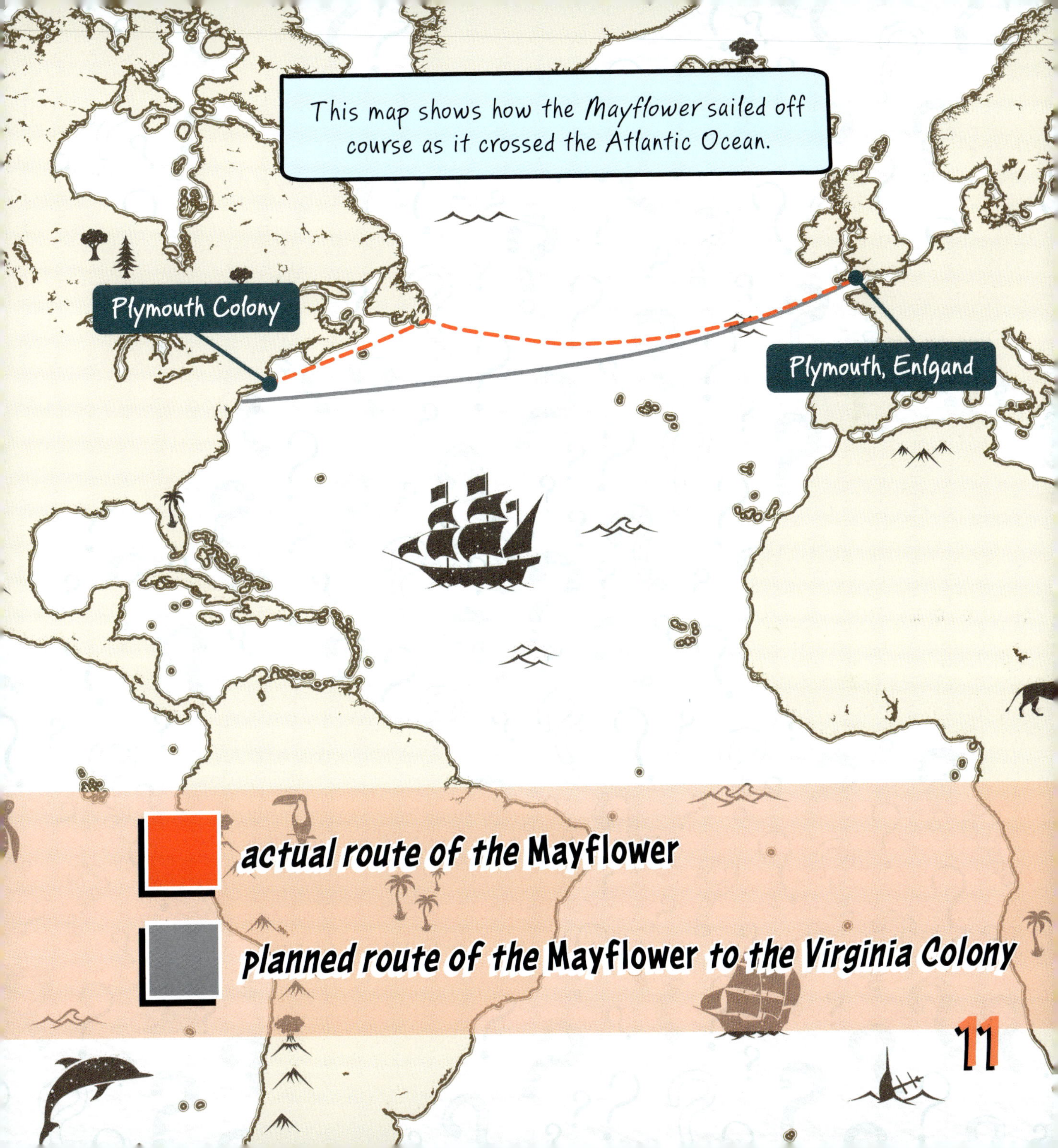

This map shows how the *Mayflower* sailed off course as it crossed the Atlantic Ocean.

QUESTION 6

Why did the leaders choose to land where they did?

ANSWER

They found a place on a hill that had been **abandoned** by a nearby Native group, the Wampanoag. It had land for farming already cleared. There was a good water supply too.

The *Mayflower* landed at Cape Cod in present-day Massachusetts in November 1620. A few weeks later, the Pilgrims had chosen the spot where Plymouth would be built.

QUESTION 7

Why did the Pilgrims need the Mayflower Compact?

ANSWER

The Separatists and other Pilgrims disagreed about whether the patent they had was void because they didn't land in Virginia. The compact bound the settlers together until a new patent could arrive. It set up laws to establish order too.

signing the Mayflower Compact

QUESTION 8

Why did the Pilgrims arrive in winter?

ANSWER

It wasn't planned. Many **delays** in leaving England caused this. No one was prepared for the cold, hard New England winter. About half these original colonists died, including three-quarters of the women.

The colonists died mostly from illness that first winter in North America.

QUESTION 9

Where did the Pilgrims live?

ANSWER

The Pilgrims had to build all their homes in the New World. They tried to prepare for this. They brought tools and nails. But, they had to cut down trees and shape the wood—and build in the wintertime!

Until March 1621, the Pilgrims mostly lived on the *Mayflower*. At that time, enough houses were built so they could move ashore.

QUESTION 10

Why name the settlement Plymouth?

ANSWER

The area had already been called Plymouth! A Jamestown Colony leader named John Smith had called it that years before on maps he made. But the Pilgrims kept the name to honor Port Plymouth, the place in England they had sailed from.

John Smith made some of the best maps of northeast North America in the early 1600s.

NATIVE NEIGHBORS

QUESTION 11

Who were the Wampanoag?

ANSWER

These Native people had made their home in northeast North America for thousands of years. The Wampanoag were made up of many communities, including the Pokanoket. Each community had its own government.

Groups of Wampanoag lived near Plymouth Colony. These were not the first Europeans they had met, however. Years before, European **explorers** brought illnesses to the Wampanoag that killed many.

QUESTION 12

Why was Tisquantum important?

ANSWER

He was a Patuxet who helped the Pilgrims talk to the Wampanoag who lived near their settlement. Tisquantum helped the Pilgrim's governor John Carver make a peace agreement with the Pokanoket leader, Ousamequin, or Massasoit.

Tisquantum, sometimes called Squanto, also taught the Pilgrims how to grow corn and other North American crops.

QUESTION 13

Who was William Bradford?

ANSWER

Bradford took over as governor when Carver died in 1621. He led the colony for 30 years! He kept a **detailed** journal, which was called *Of Plymouth Plantation* when it was printed. Historians have learned a lot about the colony from his writing!

William Bradford

QUESTION 14

Why did the first Thanksgiving happen?

ANSWER

The Pilgrims had a good harvest in the fall of 1621. Their Native neighbors had a lot to do with this success! So, the two groups gathered to celebrate the harvest. Ousamequin and about 90 other Wampanoag came.

first Thanksgiving reenactment

THE FIRST THANKSGIVING MEAL

venison

corn bread

fowl

These are just some of the foods that are likely to have been at this harvest celebration. It's possible turkey was served at the first Thanksgiving, but the **fowl** served may have been duck or goose.

beans

squash

shellfish

SELF-SUFFICIENCY

QUESTION 15

Were the colonists new to farming?

ANSWER

It's unlikely the colonists had ever farmed before founding Plymouth! They called their settlement Plymouth Plantation, or large farm. The Pilgrims grew pumpkins, beans, wheat, and more, as well as Indian corn.

The Pilgrims called the corn the Wampanoag taught them to farm Indian corn. It's not the kind you eat off the cob! This corn was dried and ground into cornmeal.

QUESTION 16

Why was farming so important?

ANSWER

First of all, farming allowed the colonists to feed themselves. Secondly, they traded their extra crops to the Native people for furs. These furs were sold in England. Later on, this money bought the colonists sugar, oil, spices, shoes, and even gunpowder!

QUESTION 17

Was Plymouth Colony successful?

ANSWER

For the first few years, the Plymouth colonists had to fulfill the agreement with their investors. But by 1627, Bradford set up a way to pay off the colony's **debts**. Settlers were given their own land. The colony was growing!

In 1627, about 160 people lived in Plymouth Colony. Some had come over on other ships that arrived after the *Mayflower*.

QUESTION 18

What was a child's life like in Plymouth Colony?

ANSWER

Children worked hard in Plymouth. They worked in their family's corn fields. They cooked and took care of animals. Older children watched their younger brothers and sisters too.

The Pilgrims brought farm animals to North America on the *Mayflower*. Children cared for them, among other chores. They had some time to play too though.

GROWING COLONIES

QUESTION 19

When was the Massachusetts Bay Colony founded?

ANSWER

About 1,000 Puritan colonists from England founded it around 1630. The New Haven Colony, Connecticut Colony, and Rhode Island Colony were also founded around this time by different groups of Puritans.

This map shows the growth of Plymouth Colony as well as where the Massachusetts Bay Colony grew up in present-day Massachusetts.

QUESTION 20

What was King Philip's War?

ANSWER

As colonies grew in New England, Native groups and colonists fought over land. In 1675, Ousamequin's son Metacom led Wampanoag and other Native Americans against the colonists. Thousands died—and the colonists won.

The colonists called Metacom King Philip. Fighting didn't last long after he was killed in August 1676.

MASSACHUSETTS COLONY

As time went on, Plymouth's colonists moved away from the original settlement. They formed more communities. They moved away from their close religious group. Then, in 1691, Plymouth became part of the Massachusetts Colony, along with the Massachusetts Bay Colony.

Today, you can visit the Plimouth Patuxet Museum in Plymouth, Massachusetts. It features a recreated town based on Plymouth Colony. There is also a recreated Patuxet settlement where visitors can learn about life among the Wampanoag in the 1600s.

There's no better way to learn about Plymouth Colony than to visit the Plimouth Patuxet Museum.

GLOSSARY

abandoned: Having to do with being empty and uncared for.

cargo: Goods carried by a boat, train, or other vehicle.

celebrate: To honor with special activities.

cramped: The state of being close together.

debt: Money owed.

delay: Stops or slowdowns.

detailed: Having many small parts.

explorer: Someone who searches to find a new place.

fowl: Birds, like turkeys and geese, that are eaten as food.

New England: The northeastern part of the present-day United States.

patent: An official paper that gives a person or group the rights to a piece of land.

FOR MORE INFORMATION

BOOKS

Connors, Kathleen. *Q & A About Colonial America*. Buffalo, NY: Enslow Publishing, 2025.

Hansen, Grace. *Living in Colonial America.* Minneapolis, MN: Pop!, 2024.

WEBSITES

Colonial America
https://www.ducksters.com/history/colonial_america/
Find out about how the North American colonies were founded.

Plimoth Patuxet Museums
https://plimoth.org/plan-your-visit/explore-our-sites/17th-century-english-village
Discover the early colonies and Native groups in New England—and plan a visit to learn more!

Publisher's note to educators and parents: Our editors have carefully reviewed these websites to ensure that they are suitable for students. Many websites change frequently, however, and we cannot guarantee that a site's future contents will continue to meet our high standards of quality and educational value. Be advised that students should be closely supervised whenever they access the internet.

INDEX

Bradford, William, 19, 24

Carver, John, 18

farming, 12, 18, 20, 22, 23, 25

King Philip's War, 27

Massachusetts Bay Colony, 26, 28

Mayflower, 4, 7, 8, 9, 11, 12, 15, 24, 25

Mayflower Compact, 13

Metacom, 27

New England, 4, 14, 27

Of Plymouth Plantation, 19

Ousamequin (Massasoit), 18, 20, 27

Plimouth Patuxet Musuem, 28, 29

Pokanoket, 17, 18

religion, 4, 6, 8, 28

Speedwell, 7

Thanksgiving, 4, 20, 21

Tisquatum (Squanto), 18

Virginia Colony, 10, 11, 13

Wampanoag, 4, 12, 17, 18, 20, 22, 27, 28